£5.25

Choosing pictures for
the Ryan Giggs Annual

Hello! For a soccer crazy kid (like I was!) one of the great thrills at Christmas
– or at any other time, come to that – is to receive a football annual. I used to
get the lot – Shoot, Match, Roy of the Rovers and, of course, anything to do with
my favourite team Manchester United – you name it, I read it. Those annuals kept
me going well into the New Year and beyond. I was always dipping into them,
studying the photos and reading over and over again the stories about my favourite
players. And I would secretly hope that my own picture would appear in football
annuals of the future.

Well, it worked out for me – I did become a professional footballer and pictures of
me have appeared in many football publications in the last four or five years. And now,
with the help of my friends at Grandreams, I've produced
an annual of my own. I hope you enjoy the
OFFICIAL RYAN GIGGS ANNUAL, and I hope
it keeps you entertained – just like my own
collection of soccer publications used to do for me!

Happy reading – and enjoy your football!

CONTENTS

Written by Ryan Giggs
and Tony Lynch
Edited by
Melanie J. Clayden
Designed by
Louise Ivimy.

© 1995 Grandreams
Limited.
Giggsy is a
trademark of
Ryan Giggs
Limited.

Published by
Grandreams Ltd
Jadwin House,
205–211 Kentish Town Road,
London NW5 2JU.

Printed in Italy
All facts believed correct at time of going to press.

This is the spot from where I watched my first game at Old Trafford. My dad took me. It was a First Division match between United and Sunderland in 1980. I remember the Welsh international Mickey Thomas was in the United side, wearing the No. 11 shirt. I was thrilled because I'd actually been to Old Trafford at last. I still get a buzz whenever I come here...

THE RED ZONE

Peter Schmeichel is very professional and is always willing to train. He's a fine example for all aspiring 'keepers

PETER SCHMEICHEL

RED SQUAD FACTS – PETER SCHMEICHEL

Born:	Glodsone, Denmark 18.11.1968
Height:	6' 4"
Weight:	13 06
Clubs:	Brondby, Manchester United Danish international

When I was asked to describe Peter Schmeichel in a single word, I chose the word 'massive'. Whenever I face up to Peter in the penalty-area during shooting practice, it looks as though the goal is half its normal size.

He's so dominating, and seems to cover all of the net, and that makes it difficult to decide just where to place the ball. He is very agile too, for such a big man, and the chances are that even if you do strike a good shot, he'll get to it somehow.

His brilliant distribution has brought an extra dimension to Manchester United's play. His accuracy often turns defence into attack and he seems able to throw the ball almost as far as he can kick it.

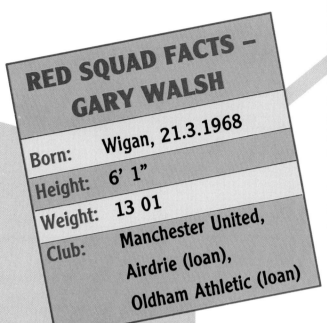

RED SQUAD FACTS – GARY WALSH

Born:	Wigan, 21.3.1968
Height:	6' 1"
Weight:	13 01
Club:	Manchester United, Airdrie (loan), Oldham Athletic (loan)

Because United play so many games in a season, it's vital that Alex Ferguson has a squad that has strength in depth. A good example of this is in the goalkeeping department. Gary Walsh – Peter Schmeichel's understudy – is a great 'keeper in his own right. If he was at any other club, he'd probably be in the first team week-in and week-out.

Walshy was in the England set-up when he was 21 or 22, but he's been really unlucky with injury and was out of the game for two or three years. It must be very frustrating for him – playing a few games here and there, and knowing that Peter is going to come back. But that's how a great club survives – with strength in depth.

GARY WALSH

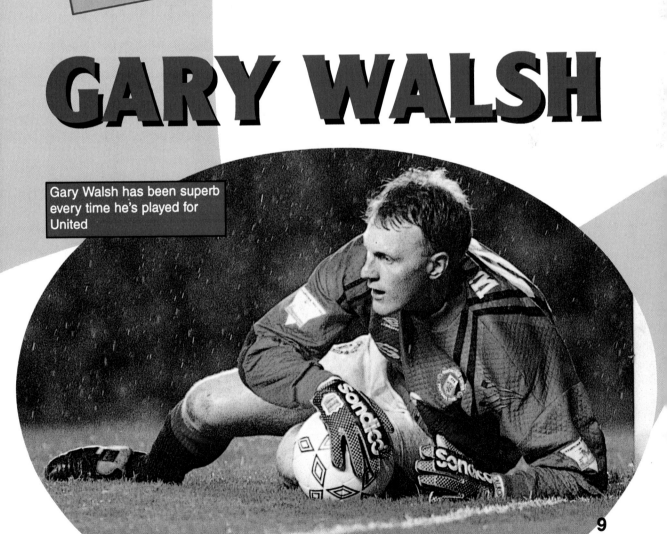

Gary Walsh has been superb every time he's played for United

I first met Alex Ferguson in my front room when he called round to ask my mum if I'd like to become an associate schoolboy player with Manchester United. Did I? You bet I did!

Since I was ten or eleven I'd been training with Manchester City, who at that time had the best scouting system in the north-west. City were renowned for bringing youngsters through the ranks. But when Alex Ferguson arrived at Old Trafford in 1986, he changed that situation. He revitalised United's youth policy and nowadays we are seeing the results of his efforts with a number of teenagers breaking into the first team – just like I did. Now I believe he has got the right blend of experienced players bought on the transfer market and young players who have come through the system

He is a brilliant Boss. He really looks after

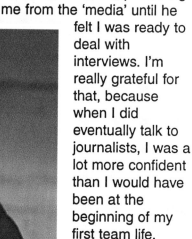

Alex Ferguson became the first manager to win the three major honours on both sides of the border. He has also achieved European Cup Winners' Cup success with both Aberdeen and Manchester United.

the youngsters and always seems to have time for you, whoever you are. When I played for the 'B' team, he would often come down and chat with my mum and the other parents on the touchline. I think he's created a real family atmosphere at the club.

He looked after me more or less from the start, protecting me from the 'media' until he felt I was ready to deal with interviews. I'm really grateful for that, because when I did eventually talk to journalists, I was a lot more confident than I would have been at the beginning of my first team life.

The Gaffer is quite a disciplinarian. He certainly lets you know when you've done something he doesn't agree with. But all great mangers are like that, and in Alex Ferguson's case it has brought brilliant success to Manchester United...

ALEX FERGUSON- THE GAFFER

FERGIE FACTS

Born: Govan, 31.12.1941

Playing Career: Queen's Park, St Johnstone, Dunfermline, Rangers, Falkirk, Ayr United, East Stirling

Managerial Career: St Mirren, Aberdeen, Scottish national team, Manchester United

Me, The Boss and some silverware

11

Catching up on the Premiership facts and figures

So this is what they meant by 'signing for Man United'!

THE RED SQUAD

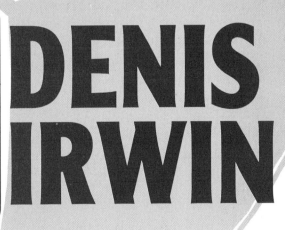

Denis is Manchester United's 'Mr Consistent'. He never has a bad game, never rates less that 8 out of 10 and never lets you down. A world class attacking defender, his timing is perfect and his tackling precise.

Denis is deceptively fast and he scores lots of important goals – such as his two against Wrexham in the Fourth Round of the FA Cup last January. He has a brilliant right foot and is a lethal taker of free-kicks.

Apart from starring for Man United, Denis has also been a vital member of Jack Charlton's Republic of Ireland team which has done so well in recent seasons.

Denis Irwin evades a tackle by QPR's Trevor Sinclair

RED SQUAD FACTS – DENIS IRWIN

Born:	Cork, 31.10.1965
Height:	5' 8"
Weight:	11 00
Clubs:	Leeds United
	Oldham Athletic
	Manchester United
	Republic of Ireland international

DENIS IRWIN

If 'Brucie' and 'Pally' play well, then Manchester United plays well. Their central defensive partnership is the solid foundation on which the team is built and had been the most consistent element in the side for the past two or three seasons. They are also very effective in corner kick and free kick situations in the opposing penalty area.

United's captain, Steve Bruce

Steve is the Club Captain, a role he inherited from Bryan Robson. I know people say he's getting on a bit now, but his experience and example are vital to the side – and you really need someone like that in a team.

Steve is a very courageous player and is never afraid to go in where it hurts. Like Denis Irwin he scores lots of important goals – especially from set-pieces. He's very dangerous with his headers and he's an expert from the penalty-spot. In 1991 when we won the European Cup-Winners' Cup his eleven successful spot-kicks helped his season's tally to seventeen goals in all competitions.

One thing that still amazes me, and everyone else at Old Trafford, is why Steve has never been selected for England. I expected him to get picked by Graham Taylor but it never happened. And there have been times when it's seemed obvious that he and Gary Pallister would have been an ideal partnership at international level as well as club level.

RED SQUAD FACTS – STEVE BRUCE	
Born:	Newcastle, 31.12.1960
Height:	6' 0"
Weight:	12 06
Clubs:	Gillingham, Norwich City, Manchester United

STEVE BRUCE

Gary is a big strong lad, standing around 6' 4". Yet for a such a tall person he's got really good feet. I've never seen anyone out-sprint Pally – I reckon he's the quickest defender around. His height is a great advantage too, not many players can beat him in the air.

He is an established England international now and that experience has made him an even better player.

I don't envy any attackers squaring up to Brucie and Pally...I'm just glad they're on my side!

RED SQUAD FACTS – GARY PALLISTER

Born:	Ramsgate, 30.6.1965
Height:	6' 4"
Weight:	13 04
Clubs:	Middlesbrough, Darlington (loan), Manchester United

England international

& GARY PALLISTER

Gary Pallister is the Big Man at the back for United

THE RED ZONE

DID YOU KNOW...?

🔱 The record attendance at Old Trafford is 76,962 – and United weren't even playing in the match. It was an FA Cup semi-final between Wolves and Grimsby Town on 25 March 1939. Wolves won 5–0, but they lost in the Final against Portsmouth at Wembley!

🔱 The record Old Trafford attendance for a match involving United is 70,504, against Aston Villa on 27 December 1920. Villa won 3–1!

🔱 United's biggest League victory was 10–1, against Wolves in October 1892!

The Gaffer's place. This is where Alex Ferguson sits on matchdays – alongside his assistant Brian Kidd.

17

OPPONENTS!

Among the trickiest defenders I've come up against while playing for United are Earl Barrett of Aston Villa (now Everton) and Gary Kelly (left) of Leeds United.

18

Nottingham Forest's Stan Collymore proved his worth with some brilliant strikes and Bryan Roy brought a touch of continental class to England.

In 1994–95 Chris Sutton answered all those critics who said that even with his £5 million price tag, he wouldn't be able to play alongside Alan Shearer. He answered them in the best possible way – with a whole hatful of goals.

Alan Shearer was quite brilliant for Rovers in 1994–95, scoring several hat-tricks and supplying several contenders for 'Goal of the Season'.

On the international scene Romania's midfield general Ghorghe Hagi is one of the best players I've ever seen. He scored twice and really ran the show in a 5–1 defeat of Wales in a World Cup qualifier in May 1992.

Andy Cole, United's £7 million superstriker

I was as surprised as everyone else when it was announced in January '95 that Andy Cole was joining Manchester United. But the move was just another example of Alex Ferguson's shrewd eye for the transfer market.

Andy's goalscoring record for Newcastle speaks for itself and every Premiership club must have envied The Magpies, just as they must now envy Man United.

I knew Andy was fast, but I didn't realise just how fast until his second game for United against Crystal Palace. At one point I was sprinting pretty fast as we mounted an attack, and he went past me like a rocket!

When Andy first came to United a lot of articles were written, comparing his style to that of Mark Hughes and saying he couldn't possibly do the same job as Sparky does for the club. I think that's a bit unfair as they are completely different players. Mark likes to hold the ball up and depends on his strength, whereas Coley is a much quicker player who relies on speed.

We were all relieved when Andy scored his first goal for United, against Aston Villa.

There have been more since then and I'm sure there will be many, many more to come.

Andy Cole, United's £7 million superstriker

RED SQUAD FACTS – ANDY COLE

Born:	Nottingham, 15.10.1971
Height:	5' 11"
Weight:	11 02
Clubs:	Arsenal, Fulham (loan), Bristol City (loan), Bristol City, Newcastle United, Manchester United

Sparky takes a pot–shot against Leeds

RED SQUAD FACTS – MARK HUGHES

Born:	Wrexham, 1.11.1963
Height:	5' 9"
Weight:	11 12
Clubs:	Manchester United, Barcelona, Bayern Munich (loan), Manchester United Welsh international

When I was a kid Mark Hughes was definitely one of my favourite players. And, having played alongside 'Sparky' in so many matches for United and Wales, he remains one of my all–time favourite players. He's just so strong and so tough. He depends on that strength, especially when he's holding the ball up, as he loves to do.

Mark is one of the bravest players I've ever seen. He's never afraid to go in where it hurts. That was proved when he was stretchered off last January after colliding with Pavel Srnicek while scoring against Newcastle. The gashed knee kept Sparky out for several weeks.

He's so competitive, even in training. We try to get the ball off him, but it's impossible!

When Andy Cole arrived at Old Trafford the Press predicted that Mark would soon move on. I'm glad to report they were wrong – Mark signed a new two year contract with the club.

After worshipping 'Sparky' Hughes from the Stretford End when I was a kid, I was lucky enough to play alongside him for United and for Wales

21

I was born in Wales, but I captained the England Schoolboys team – why?

Well, whatever your nationality, at Schoolboy level you play for the country in which you go to school, and I went to school in Manchester. It's as simple as that.

But I am Welsh through and through, and there was never any doubt in my mind that if ever I reached international level then I would wear the red strip of my homeland.

I was selected for my one and only Wales Under–21 appearance, against Poland in May 1991 and we won 2–1.

THE WELSH

I was really chuffed and proud that day.

Five months later I was even prouder when I became – at 17 years and 322 days – the youngest-ever senior Welsh international, coming on as a substitute for Eric Young in the European Championship qualifier against Germany in Nuremberg on 16 October 1991. Mind you, I only played for a few minutes and hardly got a sniff of the ball, what with Voller, Moller, Brehme, Effenberg and Matthaus all playing for Germany – and our own Dean Saunders being sent off. Germany won 4–1.

My first game in the starting line-up for Wales was a World Cup qualifier at home against Belgium in March 1993. It was brilliant – we won 2–0 and I scored the opening goal in the eighteenth minute.

Celebrating a Welsh goal with Ian Rush

In 1994 we came close to qualifying for the World Cup finals in the USA, but we blew it at the last ditch and Romania went through instead. Most recently we've been involved in the European Championship qualifiers for the 1996 Finals in England.

Now that our management problems have been resolved, I hope the Welsh national team can look to a more positive future...

Mark Hughes in action against Belgium

CONNECTION

MAGIC MO

I've got my hands on the FA Cup after United completed the 'double' by beating Chelsea 4–0 at Wembley in 1994

Me, Brucie and Sharpy celebrate winning the League Cup in 1992

MENTS!

Lifting the Premier League trophy in 1993

Scoring against Spurs at White Hart Lane

Flashback to 1992: Gary Pallister is PFA Player of the Year, and I am the Young Player of the Year

25

THE RED ZONE

This used to be the tunnel where the teams ran out on matchdays...

...Now we've got new dressing rooms and a new covered tunnel

DID YOU KNOW...?

Ψ The first game played at Old Trafford was Manchester United v Liverpool on 19 February 1910. United lost 4–3. The club had previously played at two other grounds – North Road in Monsall and Bank Street in Clayton!

Ψ The first floodlit match at Old Trafford was played on 25 March 1957. United may have lost 2–0 to Bolton, but they went on to lift a second successive Championship!

Ψ Before becoming 'Manchester United', the club was known as Newton Heath. The change was made in 1902!

ANDREI KANCHELSKIS

Andrei Kanchelskis, the man with the rocket shot

It's smiles all round for Andrei and me

RED SQUAD FACTS – ANDREI KANCHELSKIS

Born: Kirowgrad, Russia, 23.1.1969

Height: 5' 10"

Weight: 12 04

Clubs: Dynamo Kiev, Donezts, Manchester United Russian international

Andrei Kanchelskis has had a real surge of confidence lately and it has made him an even better player. Not only is he very, very quick, he's also very strong and has the hardest shot of anyone at Old Trafford.

He is a great favourite with the Manchester United fans – they just love to see him running at the opposing defence. I reckon it was their influence which persuaded him to stay with United a few months ago.

D SQUAD
& DAVID MAY

RED SQUAD FACTS – DAVID MAY

Born:	Oldham, 24.6.1970
Height:	6' 0"
Weight:	11 07
Clubs:	Blackburn Rovers, Manchester United

David's arrival at Old Trafford came as a great surprise - a surprise in the same way that Eric Cantona's arrival had been a couple of years earlier.

The Gaffer signed Eric from Leeds after we'd given them a close race in the 1991–92 title race. Likewise, he signed David from Blackburn after they had given us a torrid time in the 1993–94 campaign.

David has done well since coming to Old Trafford, playing at right back, although I think he would be happier in his natural position of centre half.

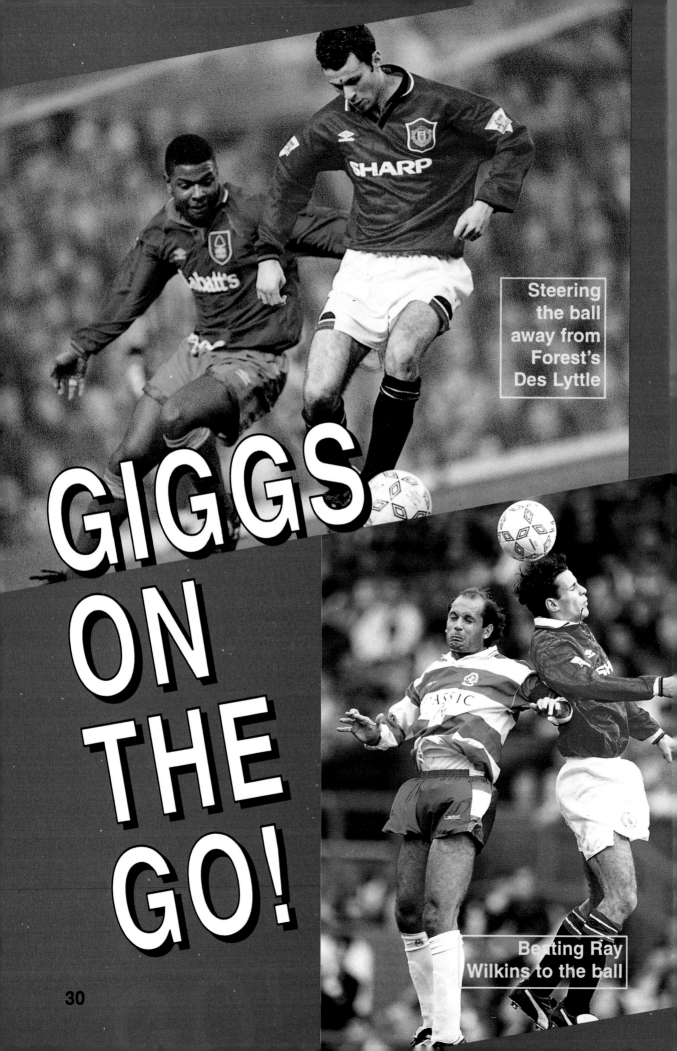

GIGGS ON THE GO!

Steering the ball away from Forest's Des Lyttle

Beating Ray Wilkins to the ball

Going over the top
against Leeds

A tough time
at Tottenham

THE RED SQUAD

Brian is the brainy one in the United squad, complete with a university degree. He's one of those people who will tell a joke that's so clever, you get it about two days later!

Alex Ferguson is always reminding us of how important Brian has been to the team – he's been a brilliant player for the club since joining from Celtic in 1987. He will run all day – whether he's playing right wing, left wing, upfront, or in midfield – and he never, ever complains.

Brian is one of Old Trafford's all-time favourites, and deservedly so.

BRIAN McCLAIR & PAUL PARKER

RED SQUAD FACTS – BRIAN McCLAIR

Born:	Bellshill, 8.12.1963
Height:	5' 9"
Weight:	12 00
Clubs:	Aston Villa, Motherwell, Celtic, Manchester United Scottish international

Paul is a perfect example of Alex Ferguson's acumen when dealing in the transfer market. The Boss signed him from QPR for £1.5 million in 1991.

Before the ankle injury which kept him out for much of the 1994–95 season, Paul had proved one of United's most consistent performers. He is equally adept at centre half or right back.

RED SQUAD FACTS – PAUL PARKER

Born:	Essex, 4.4.1964
Height:	5' 7"
Weight:	10 13
Clubs:	Fulham, QPR, Manchester United England international

32

PAUL SCHOLES

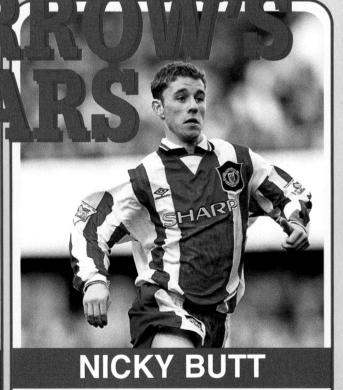

BEN THORNLEY

Paul's is a year younger than me. I used to play alongside him in the Manchester United Youth team. He has a brilliant footballing brain and is really talented. He can play equally well as an out-and-out goalgetter, or as a creative midfielder. Paul has done brilliantly since breaking into the first team last season. He scored a lot of goals very quickly and the Press began comparing him to Denis Law. Personally, I think it's a bit too early to say that, just as it was when they compared me to George Best a few seasons back.

Ben Thornley is a local lad and I know him very well. We played together in the same District team. He was on the fringe of the United first team, but unfortunately he suffered a 'Gazza' type of knee injury which has hampered his progress. Now he's playing again and hopefully will get back to full strength.

TOMORROW'S STARS

SIMON DAVIES

NICKY BUTT

I've known Simon since I was eleven – I used to play against him in Sunday League football. He played a few games on the left wing when me and Sharpy were injured last season – and he scored a really good goal for United in the European Cup last year against Galatasary.

Butty is another lad who I played alongside in the Youth side. He did well in his first season, appearing in all the European games which couldn't have been easy for him. Nicky is in the Paul Ince mould – a good tackler, a good ball winner and a great passer of the ball.

I didn't know how good Eric Cantona was – how special he was – before he came to Old Trafford from Leeds. But I soon found out, and can now say without doubt that he is quite simply the best player I've ever played with.

He is so nonchalant on the field and makes everything look so easy. He's aware of everything that's going on and his passing is just superb.

I don't think people realise just how hard Eric works in training. He'll often stay on after training has finished, to polish up his phenomenal range of skills.

English football has suited him perfectly, especially the way Manchester United play with two wingers.

I was sorry to see that incident at Crystal Palace in January '95 which effectively brought his season to a premature end and added to his controversial reputation.

Eric Cantona receives close attention from Leeds United's David White

RED SQUAD FACTS – ERIC CANTONA

Born: Paris, 25.5.1966

Height: 6' 1"

Weight: 12 10

Clubs: Auxerre, Martigues, Auxerre, Marseille, Bordeaux, Montpellier, Marseille, Nimes, Leeds United, Manchester United

France international

ERIC CANTONA

Incey is my best mate in the United team. He's a great joker and is always taking the mickey out of someone or another.

He really is a tremendous player who has come on bundles in the last few years. He arrived at Old Trafford around the same time as Gary Pallister – and I reckon they both proved to be real bargain buys.

Paul captained England against the USA in June 1993, and I believe he is also a future Manchester United skipper.

Paul Ince – always on the ball

RED SQUAD FACTS – PAUL INCE

Born:	Ilford, 21.10.1967
Height:	5' 10"
Weight:	11 07
Clubs:	West Ham United, Manchester United England international

& PAUL INCE

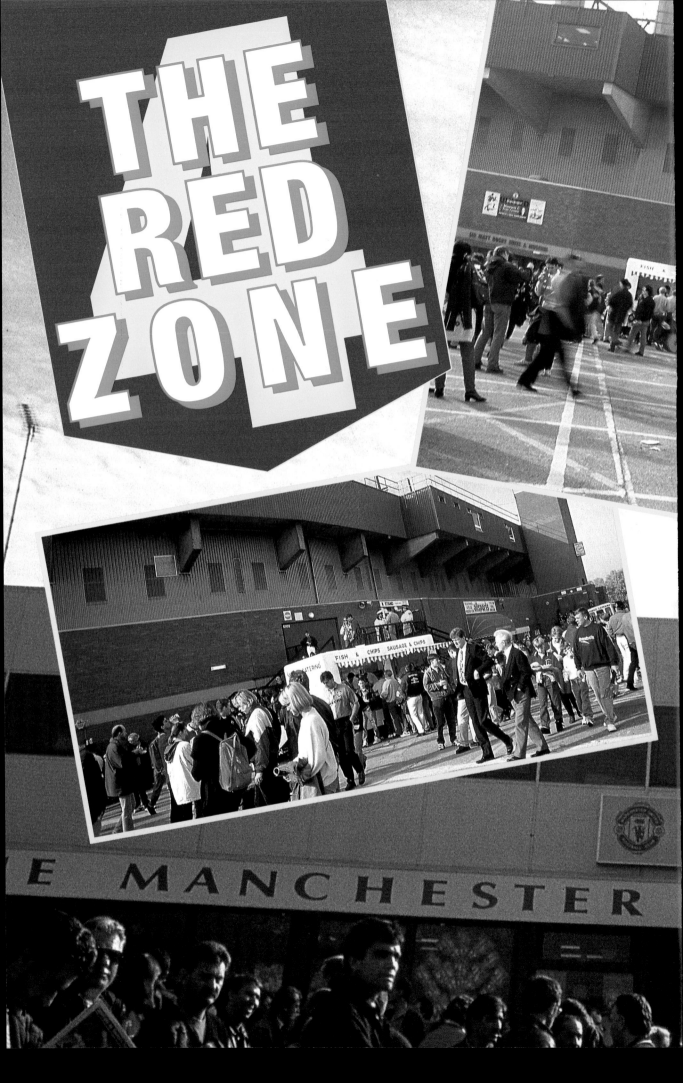

THE RED ZONE

E MANCHESTER

MANCHESTER UNITED

Old Trafford is a fantastic place to be on a match day. The atmosphere builds up as you start to approach the ground. Inside it's electric!

UNITED SUPERST

This is the Superstore at Old Trafford – it's packed with Manchester United goodies!

When Roy Keane arrived at Manchester United for £3.75 million in July '93 he was England's most expensive footballer

Keaney, or 'Damien' as he's sometimes known, is a really strong player who can run all day. He can score goals and he can get back and defend effectively as well. Last season he played a lot of games at right back which just goes to prove that he can play well in a variety of different roles.

I think Roy and Paul Ince form the very best midfield partnership in the country. Roy is really witty, always taking the mick out of people. In 1994 he never tired of reminding the rest of the team that he and Denis Irwin were off to the World Cup Finals with the Republic of Ireland – while the rest of us were staying at home!

In return, he got a lot of stick when he sprouted that little pointy 'devil's' beard a few months ago.

ROY KEANE &

RED SQUAD FACTS - ROY KEANE

Born:	Cork, 10.8.1971
Height:	5' 10"
Weight:	11 03
Clubs:	Cobh Ramblers, Nottingham Forest, Manchester United
	Republic of Ireland international

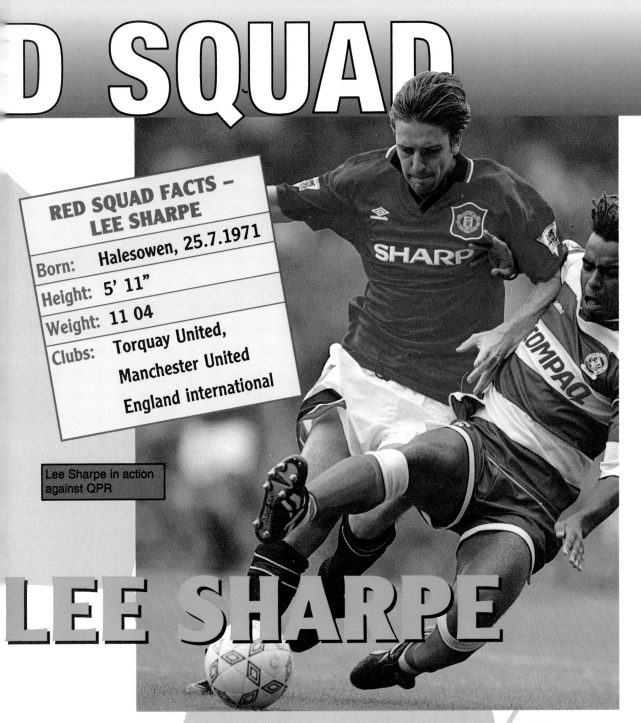

RED SQUAD FACTS –
LEE SHARPE

Born:	Halesowen, 25.7.1971
Height:	5' 11"
Weight:	11 04
Clubs:	Torquay United, Manchester United

England international

Lee Sharpe in action against QPR

LEE SHARPE

When I was an Old Trafford apprentice I played mainly on the left wing. At the same time Lee Sharpe was occupying the left wing berth in United's first team. He was so good – he won the PFA's Young Player of the Year Award in 1991 – that I started to think I'd got no chance of ever breaking into the senior line up.

In fact, it was because Lee was suffering from an injury that I made the breakthrough into the Manchester United first team.

Sharpy first arrived at Old Trafford as a 16-year-old. Alex Ferguson had heard about his exploits for Torquay United back in 1988, and he signed him for United for a bargain £125,000. Lee began as a left back, but gradually as he got bigger and stronger they realised he could play left wing as well. He really came to everyone's notice when he scored a brilliant hat-trick in United's 6–2 victory against Arsenal at Highbury, in the Fourth Round of the League Cup in November 1990.

He became an full England international at 19. A great player and a good mate!

THE LIFE OF RYAN

I've been football mad since I was about seven...and I was a Manchester United fan right from the start. My dad first took me to Old Trafford on 30 August 1980, to watch a First Division match between United and Sunderland – it ended in a 1–1 draw. The Yugoslavian player Nicky Jovanovic scored for United, but I was more interested in the man in the red No. 11 shirt, Mickey Thomas, because he was Welsh, like me.

I was born in Cardiff on Thursday 29 November 1973. We lived there until my dad signed for the Swinton Rugby League Club which meant a move to the Manchester area. I went to the Grosvenor

Playing against Forest in 1992

was a Manchester City scout and he picked three of us from the team to go along to City's School of Excellence twice a week, on Tuesdays and Thursdays. We played lots of five-a-side games and worked on different skills. In the school holidays I went every day and really got into the swing of things with the apprentices.

I moved on to the Moorside High School in Swinton, and became captain of the football team there.

The north-west is one of the great hot-beds of soccer. There are so many clubs in the area and they're constantly on the lookout for talented youngsters. I was seen by Preston, Blackburn and Blackpool, but I always thought that I'd become an associate schoolboy at Maine Road when I was fourteen. After all, Manchester City had looked after me since I was ten or eleven.

Although all this was happening to me, I didn't realise how good a player I was I was until I went to the England Schoolboys trials in Nottingham in 1988, as one of 120 hopefuls. I didn't really expect to do well as these were the very best schoolboy footballers in the country, and each time I got through a stage I expected to go out at the next one.

But I progressed step by step through the last 80, the last 40, the last 20 and then into the team itself. I eventually became captain of England Schoolboys and in the 1988–89 season we played nine games, winning seven and losing two. I also captained the Salford District Boys team in the second-leg of the 1989 English Schools Cup Final against St Helens at Old Trafford. Unfortunately we lost the match and the tie.

By then I was on the

Road Primary School which is where I first played organised football.

From there I was invited to the Deans club in Salford to play for their Under–11 Sunday League side.

The manager at Deans

books as a associate schoolboy at Manchester United. When the time had come City had not asked for my signature after all. Then United invited me to train with them for a week – and I felt at home the minute I got there.

Soon afterwards Alex Ferguson turned up at my home (I could hardly believe it, Alex Ferguson in person, in our house!) to tell my mum that he wanted to sign me as

come as a big shock when you make it to the first team. You're not overawed by it all.

On school holidays the associated schoolboys go to The Cliff, United's training ground, to mix with the first team players and train on the same field as them. After a while you just get used to being around them.

I was also lucky because I only live ten minutes way from Old Trafford and The Cliff.

a schoolboy. Mum felt it was only right to clear it with City, because they'd looked after me for so long. She checked with them, and was told they weren't interested. So I signed for United.

The Manchester United method of integrating young players into their set-up is brilliant. You are brought up within the surroundings of Old Trafford, in the Big Club atmosphere, so it doesn't

I had all the comforts of home and never had to go away and live in digs like a lot of young players.

I rose through the schoolboy ranks under the watchful eyes of coaches Brian Kidd, Nobby Stiles and Eric Harrison. I got on well with all of them. I played in the 'B' and 'A' teams and while still only 14 came on as a substitute in the reserve team against Everton reserves

Celebrating a United goal

towards the end of the season. It was quite an experience, actually playing against men.

At 16 I was offered a YTS Traineeship and grabbed the chance with both hands. Most of my games were in the 'A' team with just a handful of games in the reserves.

Then one Friday in March 1991, when I was 17, Brian Kidd told me I'd be training with the first team for that weekend's game against Everton. I thought it was just another way of giving a young player some more valuable experience, another part of the integration process. I certainly didn't expect to play in the game, but when I was named as one of the subs it obviously became a real possibility.

Running out of the tunnel to be greeted by 45,000 fans was just brilliant. I was nervous, to say the least, while sitting on the bench. But I was raring to go, and was really pleased when Alex Ferguson sent me on in place of Denis Irwin. We lost the match 2–0, but I was a real Manchester United player at last.

My next first team appearance came two months later. I was in the starting line-up in the local derby against Man City. In the 22nd minute I was involved in a goalmouth scramble in which I was struck by the ball which then rebounded off Colin Hendry and went into the net. It went into the record books as my first goal for Manchester United – and it was the only goal of the game.

Lee Sharpe was injured at the beginning of the 1991–92 season, and for that reason I got my chance to fill the left-wing berth for most of the campaign. We were going really well too, and were favourites to win the First Division Championship. But, as everyone now knows, we

43

lost out to Leeds United following two dismal performances against West Ham and Liverpool in the run-in to the end of the season.

We did win the League Cup in 1991–92, beating Nottingham Forest 1–0 at of the year were top of the table. It became a two horse race after that and we eventually outpaced Aston Villa to win the title.

It was Manchester United's first Championship since 1967 and everyone in the Red Zone went games in the Premiership campaign, two against Chelsea and one each against Blackburn and Wimbledon. Altogether we accumulated 92 points (six more than in the previous season) to win the title ahead of Blackburn and Newcastle.

Ball control – showing Incey how it's done!

Wembley, and I was voted PFA Young Player of the Year – a great honour, especially as those doing the voting were my fellow professionals.

The new Premier League arrived in 1992–93 – and so did Manchester United. We had a lot to prove after the disappointment of the previous season. And this time things went according to plan.

After a decidedly dodgy start – two defeats and a draw – we began to get our act together and by the turn completely bonkers for a while. We were already confirmed as Champions when we met Blackburn at Old Trafford on 3 May. We won the match 3–1 and it turned into one great big party as we collected our medals and that all-important Premiership trophy. I was again voted Young Player of the Year by the PFA membership – it was the first time anyone had won that honour twice.

As if that wasn't enough, things got even better in 1993–94. United lost just four We also reached the FA Cup Final at Wembley to make the elusive 'double' a distinct possibility. Only five other clubs had ever achieved the feat – Preston, Aston Villa, Tottenham, Arsenal and Liverpool – would Manchester United be added to the list?

First we had to take on Chelsea – the only team to beat us twice earlier in the season. For most of the first half it looked as though the Blues were going to do it again. They were definitel the dominant side and

Eyes on
the ball

way. Five minutes later we
had a second penalty – which
was hotly disputed by the
Chelsea players. Once again
Eric strode up and put the ball
past Dmitri, to put us two-up.

After that our nerves
seemed to settle a bit and we
were able to play a more fluid
game. Two more goals from
Mark Hughes and Brian
McClair put the result beyond
doubt. United had won the
coveted 'double' and I was as
pleased and as proud as I
could possibly be.

On the ball
against
Liverpool

almost went ahead, but luckily
Gavin Peacock's twenty-yarder
struck Peter Schmeichel and
rebounded harmlessly off the
crossbar.

After a bit of half time
reorganisation by Alex
Feguson, we came out
determined to win it in the
second half. The deadlock was
finally broken after an hour of
play, when Denis Irwin was
fouled in the Chelsea penalty
box and Eric Cantona
converted the kick from the
spot while causing Dmitri
Kharine to dive the wrong